MW00774345

ક&

Presented to

_____

by

_____

on

_____

THE
GRANDMA'S ATTIC
COOKBOOK

THE GRANDMA'S ATTIC
COOKBOOK

Arleta Richardson

Chariot Books™
David C. Cook Publishing Co.

Chariot Books is an imprint of David C. Cook Publishing Co.
David C. Cook Publishing Co., Elgin, Illinois 60120
David C. Cook Publishing Co., Weston, Ontario
Nova Distribution Ltd., Torquay, England

THE GRANDMA'S ATTIC COOKBOOK
© 1993 by Arleta Richardson

All rights reserved. Except for brief excerpts for review purposes, no part of this book may be
reproduced or used in any form without written permission from the publisher.

Cover and internal design by Helen Lannis
Cover illustration by Dora Leder

First printing, 1993
Printed in the United States of America
97 96 95 94 93   5 4 3 2 1

Library of Congress Cataloging-in-Publication Data
Richardson, Arleta.
The Grandma's attic cookbook / by Arleta Richardson.
        p.   cm.
ISBN 0-7814-0065-1
1. Cookery. I. Title.
TX714.R517 1993
641.5—dc20

                                                        93-3132
                                                         CIP

Dedicated to the Corser sisters,
who have been a joy
and
an inspiration

Ruth Corser Stewart (1903-1992), a special friend whose
wonderful soup made being ill worth the misery

Margaret Corser Green, a gracious hostess who knows the
blessing of the little extras, and gives them so selflessly

Catherine Corser Jensen, a loyal friend who loves and
spreads beauty through a Christlike life

Table of Contents

Grandma's Recipes

❧

Her cookies were the best ones made.

No one could match her lemonade.

She cured the best of country ham

And made delicious berry jam.

A better pie no one could make

Nor even match her chocolate cake.

Her pickles were so crisp and nice.

Her peaches were just right with spice.

And when I'd ask her recipe,

She'd smile and shake her head at me.

"Oh, I guess at it, my dear."

And now it seems to me quite clear,

One thing she used all else above,

Her main ingredient was love.

ESTER LLOYD DAUBER

Introduction

When Grandma was growing up, all of the cooking was done on a wood range or over the fireplace. There were no gas or electric stoves to prepare meals for the family. Something as amazing as the microwave oven was not even dreamed of!

There were no such things as biscuit or cake mixes, ready-to-spread frosting, or freezer dinners. You gathered all the ingredients for your meals from the garden and the orchard, and if you didn't have something, you either did without it, substituted something else, or changed your menu. There was no short run to the supermarket for a forgotten item!

Nevertheless, most older people will assure you that food tasted better back then. "Not all the ladies in the community were good cooks," they will tell you, "but my mother was!" Then you will need to hear about a favorite spring meal, wash-day soup, or raspberry vinegar.

Very few recipes, or receipts as they called them, were actually written down, perhaps because a pinch, a pat, or a handful was hard to define. But grandmothers and mothers taught daughters and granddaughters the secrets that they had learned over the years, and wonderful meals and fond memories were the result.

Here are some of the favorite foods I remember from childhood, prepared as Grandma fixed them in the old farm kitchen. Oh, I know. You could make these meals much faster now. But you couldn't make them better!

arm people are busy—sometimes around the clock! On Grandma's farm there were not a lot of mechanical gadgets to hurry things along, so one thought ahead and made plans for the hours. Anything that could be done the night before was never left until morning. It would have taken a young farm wife a long time to learn this kind of organization if she hadn't grown up watching her mother do it!

The Day Begins

Breakfast was a serious occasion in Grandma's house. There was no such thing as pouring a bowl of cold cereal or grabbing a doughnut and running with it. Before one was allowed to depart for the field or for school, it was necessary to eat a hearty breakfast. A typical morning meal would look like this:

- *Fruit—fresh or sauce*
- *Hot cereal*
- *Slices of ham or bacon*
- *Sausage and eggs*
- *Fried potatoes*
- *Hash browns or pancakes or hot rolls and jam*
- *Coffee or cocoa*

Hot Cereal

1 pint water
1 teaspoon salt
1/2 cup slow-cooking oats or cornmeal

Bring water and salt to a brisk boil in top of double boiler. Slowly add cereal without stopping the boiling of the water. (Add 1/3 cup cold water to cornmeal before pouring. This will avoid lumps.)

Stir and boil in top of double boiler for five minutes.

Set pan in lower part of double boiler containing boiling water. Cover, push to the back of the stove, and cook on low heat for 45 minutes. Turn off heat and let covered pan sit on stove overnight. Bring the cereal back to a boil in the morning before serving.

I always hoped there would be lots of cornmeal mush left over, because Grandma would mold it in a glass dish, let it stand in the cooler to get firm, then slice and fry it for the noon meal. Crispy outside, with butter and syrup—umm!

But beware—nothing is hotter than cornmeal mush!

To have either delicious oatmeal or cornmeal for breakfast, Grandma would use the double boiler.

Fear not for tomorrow. God is already there.

Another breakfast favorite was Grandma's buckwheat pancakes.

Overnight Raised Buckwheat Cakes

1/2 package yeast (about 1 1/2 teaspoons)
1 quart warm water
1/2 cup sugar
1 cup white flour
2 cups buckwheat flour
3 teaspoons salt
pinch of soda

Dissolve yeast in water. Stir all ingredients except soda into yeast mixture until you have a smooth batter. Let set overnight in cooler. Before using, add a pinch of soda. If thinner cakes are desired, add cold water.

These pancakes are delicious with butter alone, or scrumptious with bacon drippings. (My mother turned up her nose at that, but Grandma and I loved it.)

I always had hot syrup, jam, or honey on my last pancake only. I've no idea why . . . nor did I have an answer to Uncle Roy's question: "How do you know you haven't gone past the last one?"

Learn from the mistakes of others; you may not live long enough to make them all yourself.

Fruit Sauce

With the exception of lemons, citrus fruit wasn't easy to come by in the Michigan of my childhood. Oranges, grapefruit, and limes were expensive and, though sometimes given to invalids, were not deemed necessary for well folks. Homegrown fruit, fresh or dried, made the fruit sauce we enjoyed.

In the summer, juicy apples and pears, cherries, plums, grapes, peaches, and apricots were combined for fruit cups. In winter, dried apples, prunes, apricots, and pears were stewed with a cinnamon stick and enjoyed hot or cold for any meal. The juice might be thickened with a little cornstarch or tapioca. Special on a bowl of hot cereal, too!

Grandma's Coffee

2 tablespoons ground coffee for each cup of boiling water
cold water
the crushed shells of two eggs
boiling water

Mix together thoroughly the coffee, the crushed shells, and 4 tablespoons of cold water. Let stand five minutes.

Pour on boiling water, cover tightly, and let boil three or four minutes.

Move pot to back of range, pour 3 tablespoons cold water down the spout, and let stand for eight minutes. The eggshells and cold water cause the coffee grounds to settle in the bottom of the pot, leaving clear liquid.

A pot of fragrant coffee was the first thing on Grandma's stove in the morning. There was no can of regular grind coffee in her cupboard, though. Roasted coffee beans were purchased by the pound and ground fresh each morning. A white enameled pot was proper for making boiled coffee.

Grandma made cocoa or hot chocolate in a double boiler. This recipe is for two cups of cocoa.

Grandma's Cocoa

1 1/2 cups milk
4 tablespoons cocoa powder
2 tablespoons sugar
1/2 cup boiling water

Put the milk in top of double boiler to scald over hot water.

Mix cocoa, sugar, and boiling water; cook directly over the fire until smooth and glossy.

Stir the mixture into the hot milk, beat with an eggbeater, and serve with a marshmallow.

An important part of every meal, and often in between, was Grandma's bread. It was necessary to bake several times a week, because so many good things could be made from a basic bread recipe. This was another item that could be started the night before and baked fresh in the morning.

White Bread

2 packages yeast
1 teaspoon sugar
1 cup warm water
Mix together and add:
2 cups scalded milk, cooled to lukewarm
2/3 cup melted butter
3/4 cup sugar
4 teaspoons salt
8 cups flour

Mix all together to make a soft dough. Let it stand for ten or fifteen minutes.

*B*ack of the loaf is
the snowy flour
And back of the flour,
the mill.
And back of the mill is
the wheat and the
shower
And the sun and the
Father's will.
From McGuffy's Reader

*C*hristianity is bread for daily use, not cake for special occasions.

Turn the dough onto a floured surface and knead until smooth and elastic. Place in a large greased bowl, grease the top, cover with a towel, and place in cooler.

About two hours before baking, shape into loaves and place in greased pans. Let rise until double in bulk.

Bake for forty-five minutes to an hour at 400°—keep an eye on it! Bread is baked when the crust is brown and it sounds hollow when it's thumped.

Dough may be formed into dinner rolls or will magically turn into delicious cinnamon sticky buns.

Cinnamon Rolls

Roll bread dough on the floured surface in rectangular shape.

Spread with melted butter, brown sugar, cinnamon, and chopped nuts, if desired. Roll as for jelly roll and cut into slices.

In the bottom of a pan, melt butter; add brown sugar, cinnamon, and nuts. Spread evenly.

Place the cut rolls in the pan with sides touching. Let rise until double in size and bake.

Bake at 350° for 20 minutes. Turn the pan upside down on a platter as soon as it comes from the oven.

As good as Grandma's bread was, she understood what Jesus said when He told Satan that "Man does not live on bread alone, but on every word that comes from the mouth of the Lord." Grandma made sure that her family not only had the wonderful bread that came from her oven, but that they were fed daily on the "Bread of Life." Breakfast was not complete until the Bible was read and God's blessing was asked on the day ahead. We left the house warm and fed in both soul and body.

Special Meals

Wash day on Grandma's farm was just that—a whole day. There was no throwing clothes in the washer or dryer and going about your own affairs.

I loved the kitchen on wash day. The good smell of the P & G soap, starch, bluing, and Satina, mixed with the aroma of a favorite wash-day meal, kept me close to that part of the house all day.

By the time I got to the kitchen in the morning, the washing was well under way. The clothes had been sorted the evening before, and breakfast shared the range with the boiler. The white things were steaming merrily and the windows were clouded over, so that I needed to rub a spot dry if I wanted to check the weather. Before he went to the barn, Uncle Roy had set the washtubs near the stove and filled the reservoir. Water would be added to that supply several times before the day ended.

Following Grandma to the clothesline and handing the clothespins to her was my special job. Between pulling hot clothes from the boiler with a sawed-off broom handle and scrubbing them on the washboard, Grandma somehow found time to prepare a dinner, the likes of which I still cannot eat without visions of washtubs appearing before me.

This was the menu for our "Winter Wash-Day Special."

- *Bean pot soup*
- *Fresh rolls and butter*
- *Coleslaw*
- *Pickles*
- *Pie or cookies*
- *Fruit sauce*

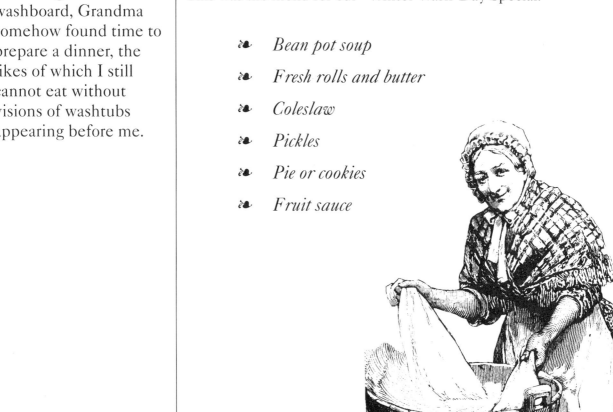

Grandma's bean soup was another start-it-the-day-before project. My job was to pick all the little stones out of the white beans, then wash them several times. The beans would then be allowed to soak in a large kettle overnight.

In the morning Grandma would drain the beans and set the kettle on top of the wood stove that heated the living room, or on the back of the range. All the ingredients were put in the kettle; then it was covered and left to its own devices for the day. If Grandma's recipe had been written down, it might have looked something like this.

Bean Pot Soup

1 lb. dried white beans
*   washed and dried*
a ham bone with scraps and
*   pieces of leftover ham*
2 1/2 quarts of water
2 onions, chopped
2 cups carrots, diced
salt and pepper

If desired, add 2 cups tomato puree late in the afternoon. (This recipe can easily be doubled. It tastes even better heated up the next day.)

I admit that I was guilty of stirring and tasting the soup several times before evening. It seemed as though someone should be testing it!

Just before time to take the wind-whipped clothes off the line, Grandma would make the coleslaw and put a pan of rolls in the oven to bake, and I would set the table. Then began the long vigil at the window until all the rest of the household returned from wherever they were, and we could sit down around the table and thank the Lord for the food He'd provided.

You say you'd rather just open a can of Campbell's and forget the fuss? Obviously, you've never had a Winter Wash-Day Special!

We may live without poetry, music, and art;
We may live without conscience and live without heart;
We may live without friends, we may live without books;
But civilized man cannot live without cooks!

Alma's Favorite Meal

Although my mother, Alma, never lived on a farm after she left to go to high school, her eating habits reflected the years of having fresh vegetables and fruit always handy. Her greatest joy was a trip to the Farmers' Market, though that was second best to going into her own garden. When she was growing up, Alma carried a saltshaker in her pocket all spring and summer. A small new carrot, onion, potato, green bean, pea pod, or tomato would be washed under the pump (or, if it was too far from the house, wiped clean on her apron!), salted, and munched happily.

It was no small wonder, then, that her favorite summer meal was simple and required little cooking. "All the sweet corn and tomatoes I can eat, with a thick slice of Mama's homemade bread," she would say. Actually, I recall one or two other items on the menu too. It looked like this.

- *New peas and potatoes creamed with chipped beef*
- *Sliced tomatoes*
- *Ears of corn*
- *Fresh bread*
- *Lemonade*

The vegetables were brought in from the garden in the order of preparation—never picked early and left lying around. While Grandma scrubbed the new potatoes and made the cream sauce, I sat on the porch and shelled the peas and husked the corn. The white sauce was the only item that needed mixing for the meal.

(Do you think people really knew what they would be missing when they moved from the country and bought a refrigerator with a vegetable crisper?)

He causes the grass to grow for the cattle and the herb for the service of men.
Psalm 104:14

White Sauce

2 tablespoons butter
2 tablespoons flour
salt and pepper
1 cup milk

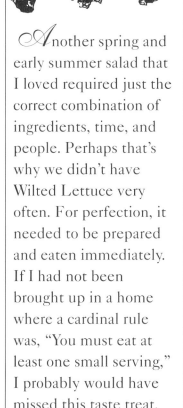

    Melt butter in a saucepan. Add flour, salt, and pepper and stir until frothy. Add cold milk slowly and stir constantly until mixture is smooth, thick, and boiling.

    Steam peas, new potatoes until tender. Tear chipped beef into small pieces and add all ingredients to white sauce. Sprinkle with paprika and parsley to serve.

    Next to the platter of sliced tomatoes, Grandma kept a bowl of vinegar, salt, and pepper into which she sliced cucumbers for each meal. They were crispy, with just the right tang for summer—and handy for snatching a few on a run through the kitchen!

Wilted Lettuce

a bowl of freshly picked leaf lettuce
bacon (7 or 8 slices)
1/2 cup vinegar

    Fry the bacon until crisp and crumble over lettuce, tossing lightly. Pour vinegar into hot bacon drippings (stand back—it splatters!). Stir a moment and pour over the lettuce. Toss again and serve at once.

    Leaf lettuce was good in other salads, on a sandwich, or just washed, shaken, and chewed down plain. But maybe best of all was helping Grandma clear the table. We would spread a little sugar along the middle veins of the leftover leaves, roll them up, and savor a "dessert." This was the best answer to the question, "What will we do with this lettuce? It won't be fresh by supper time."

Another spring and early summer salad that I loved required just the correct combination of ingredients, time, and people. Perhaps that's why we didn't have Wilted Lettuce very often. For perfection, it needed to be prepared and eaten immediately. If I had not been brought up in a home where a cardinal rule was, "You must eat at least one small serving," I probably would have missed this taste treat. I'm glad I didn't.

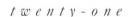

When corn was abundant in early summer, Grandma would always cook more at one time than the family could possibly eat—and that was a lot! It was amazing what she could do with the leftover corn that was cut from the cob after it was cold.

Corn Fritters

2 eggs beaten light
2/3 cup milk
2 cups corn cut from cob
1 cup flour
1 teaspoon baking powder
salt

Add milk and corn to beaten egg. Sift flour, baking powder, and salt, mix thoroughly.

Drop by spoonfuls into hot fat and fry to an amber color. Serve plain or with syrup or powdered sugar.

*C*orn on the cob tastes much better
when the tender green leaves from
the corn are used to line the bottom
of the pot while corn is cooking.

A trick my dad taught me:
Salt and pepper a pat of butter on your plate— season your corn in one motion!

Succotash

2 cups cooked lima beans
3 cups corn cut from cob
3/4 to 1 cup milk
6 tablespoons butter
salt and pepper

Heat lima beans, corn, and milk. Add the butter and seasoning. Sprinkle with paprika to serve.

Harvest Corn Pudding

2 cups corn cut from cob
1 cup milk
2 tablespoons butter
4 eggs
1 tablespoon sugar
1 tablespoon flour
1 teaspoon salt
pepper

Heat the corn, milk, and butter, but do not boil.
Beat remaining ingredients until smooth.
Slowly pour corn mixture into the eggs, then pour into baking dish.
Bake at 350° for about 45 minutes or until set and nicely browned.

God does not give us happiness. He supplies the ingredients and allows us to do the mixing.

Caramel Corn

1 cup margarine
2 cups brown sugar
1 teaspoon salt
1/2 cup corn syrup
1/2 teaspoon baking soda
1 teaspoon vanilla
peanuts (optional)
6 quarts popped corn

Heat margarine, brown sugar, salt, and corn syrup, stirring constantly until mixture boils. Cook five minutes without stirring.

Remove from heat and stir in soda and vanilla. Mix well. Add peanuts if desired. Pour over popped corn.

Spread on two large cookie sheets and bake 1 hour at 225 degrees. Stir frequently. Cool and break apart.

Roast Beef

Trim the suet from a 3-5 pound rolled roast. Cook the suet in a Dutch oven or a small roaster until brown, then remove.

Put the roast, rubbed with a little salt, into the hot fat and quickly sear it on all sides. Place the meat on a rack and add 1 cup hot water to the pan. The water should not cover the meat. Cover tightly and put in a slow oven (300-325°). Allow to roast 35-40 minutes per pound of meat.

About one hour before total cooking time is completed, add whole carrots, onions, and potatoes. (Mother rolled the potatoes in the pan drippings—they came out brown and crispy.) When tender, remove the roast and vegetables to a hot platter and keep warm on the back of the stove.

Turn the oven up to 400° and prepare Yorkshire pudding.

Aside from holiday occasions like Thanksgiving and Christmas, most every family has a favorite meal that is served on Sundays, birthdays, celebration days, or for special company. In our family it was roast beef and Yorkshire pudding, a meal done to perfection by my mother.

Yorkshire Pudding

1 egg beaten light
1 cup milk
1/4 teaspoon salt
1 cup sifted flour

Remove all but 1 cup of pan drippings from roaster and set aside for gravy. On top of the stove, bring the cup of drippings to a brisk boil and scrape the pan well.

Pour the pudding batter in and bake in hot oven about 30 minutes. The pudding will puff up like a popover and be brown around the edges.

Turn off the oven and slip the roast and vegetables in while the gravy is being made. Slice the Yorkshire pudding and serve with vegetables and gravy.

I do not recall this meal being prepared in a wood range that was not temperature controlled, but Grandma knew by putting her hand in the oven whether it was warm, moderate, or hot—and how to keep it that way—so I'm sure it could have been. The Yorkshire pudding recipe came from my Welsh father's family, and it was undoubtedly his choice dish for any special dinner.

The Fruit of Our Labor

Unless you have walked down a long row of raspberry bushes with the dust sticking to your bare legs and the sun beating down on your shoulders, and have popped a hot, red raspberry into your mouth every step or so, you do not know berries at their absolute best.

Uncle Roy cultivated raspberries for many years while I was growing up, and his daughter Marti and I spent long hours harvesting the fruit. At least, if you count stuffing ourselves and coming back to the house with a thin layer of raspberries covering the bottom of the bucket, we harvested. We always had more scratches and stains than Grandma had berries, but we also had more fun.

Since Grandma and Marti are both gone, the memories are all mine. These memories include some of the wonderful things that appeared on the table, created from the lucky berries that made it to the kitchen. These berries might be:

- *served in a bowl, covered with cream and sugar*
- *crushed and spooned over ice cream*
- *baked in pies or tarts*
- *used in filling or frosting for cake*
- *made into jam or syrup*
- *layered over shortcake and topped with whipped cream*

A favorite with the family, for any meal, was Grandma's muffins.

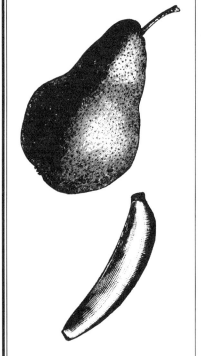

Raspberry Muffins

2 cups flour
1/2 cup sugar
1 teaspoon salt
2 teaspoons baking powder
6 tablespoons butter
1 egg
1 cup buttermilk
1 cup raspberries

Mix and sift the dry ingredients; cut in the butter.

Add slightly beaten egg and buttermilk. Carefully fold in the berries. Fill buttered muffin tins 2/3 full.

Bake at 400° for 25 minutes or until the tops are brown and have little cracks in them.

A quick-fixing dessert that tasted special was Grandma's raspberry crisp.

Raspberry Crisp

3 cups fresh raspberries
2 teaspoons lemon juice
1/3 cup butter, softened
2/3 cup brown sugar
2/3 cup rolled oats
1/2 cup flour
1 teaspoon cinnamon

Spread the berries in a baking dish and sprinkle with lemon juice.

Mix remaining ingredients and spread on top. Bake at 350° for 30 minutes or until raspberries are hot and bubbly, and topping is crispy and brown.

Serve warm or cold with ice cream or whipped cream. No leftovers—guaranteed!

The fruit of the Spirit is love, joy, peace, patience, kindness, goodness, faithfulness, gentleness and self-control. Against such things there is no law.
Galatians 5:22, 23

All of these recipes would lend themselves well to many fresh fruits in season—strawberries, peaches, blueberries, or apples. But there is one raspberry delight that I had not tasted since I was a child, and had never seen a recipe for, until recently. With the help of my friends Ruth and Heidi, this one came to light.

Raspberry Vinegar

1 pint cider vinegar
3 pints raspberries (2 cups = 1 pint)
1 pound sugar to one pint juice of raspberries

If you do not want the fruits of sin, stay out of the devil's orchard.

Wash berries and cover with vinegar. Allow to stand overnight.
Strain fruit and liquid through wet jelly bag or double cheesecloth. Add sugar and boil 15 minutes. To serve, add cold spring water to taste (approximately 1 oz. juice to 6 oz. of water). Add chips of ice, sit on the porch, and enjoy!

On the farm there were as many uses for apples as there were trees in the orchard. Pies, cobbler, baked apples, applesauce, and apples just for munching were always welcome. But when a bushel of apples stood on the porch and Grandma remarked that it was about time to make apple butter, I knew that fall was officially here. It was one of the few times when we cooked outside, and the novelty as well as the end product made this project one of the most fun events of the year.

The big black iron pot was brought in and scrubbed while the fire was started a few yards away from the house. Silver dollars were boiled to clean them thoroughly, then used to line the bottom of the pot. This was done to keep the apple butter from sticking to the pot so easily during the long cooking process. I washed the apples in the washtub, and whoever was handy helped core and slice them. By the time this was done, the fire was ready and the pot placed on it.

Apple Butter

Measure sliced apples and add an equal amount of apple cider. Allow to simmer until the apples are soft and well broken up. This will take several hours for a bushel of apples. The cooking time is well used by gathering sticks to keep the fire going at the right temperature.

Add sugar in proportion to half the amount of fruit, a few grains of salt, and spices. Grandma used cinnamon, nutmeg, and cloves. At this point the apple butter must be stirred frequently with a wooden paddle. (I was not allowed to stir this fragrant mixture, because as it thickened it would "plop" as though a stone had been thrown in, and of course it was extremely hot.)

When the mixture was thick and bubbly, Grandma tested it by dropping a spoonful on a cold saucer. If it did not separate or have a juicy rim around it, the apple butter was ready to take from the fire. Part of it was ladled into a crock and put into a cooler for immediate use. The rest was poured into hot, sterilized jars and sealed to be stored in the cellar for winter.

Nothing is quite so good as a thick slice of bread with apple butter, or a pancake smothered in the spicy preserves. And I'm sure it tastes better when you've watched the apples grow and kept the fire going while they cooked!

Remember, to be a good cook, you must know when to put it on and when to take it off.

The Ladies of the Church

Every lady knew what to prepare when the church bulletin announced a carry-in dinner, Sunday school picnic, missionary supper, or "pounding" for the pastor. This last occasion demanded not only one's prize casserole, salad, or dessert, but a food item for the pastor's pantry. Some items became mainstays—it just wouldn't be a church supper without 'em.

Mary's Bean Salad

1 cup each lima, kidney, wax, and green beans
1/2 cup each chopped onion, celery, and green pepper
Bring to boil:
1/2 cup vinegar
1/2 cup cooking oil
1 cup sugar
1 1/2 tsp. salt

   Let cool, then pour over bean mixture. Store covered in cooler for 24 hours. This dish improves with age.

Phyllis T.'s Meat Loaf
with Sweet & Sour Sauce

1 1/2 pounds ground beef
1 cup soft bread crumbs
15 ounces tomato sauce
1/2 teaspoon pepper
1/2 cup chopped onion
1 teaspoon salt

  Mix meat, bread crumbs, onion, salt, and pepper with half of the tomato sauce (save the rest for sauce below). Bake at 350° for 50 minutes.

You can't think rationally on an empty stomach. A lot of people can't do it on a full one, either.

Sweet & Sour Sauce

1/4 to 1/2 cup sugar
2 tablespoons prepared mustard
2 tablespoons brown sugar
2 tablespoons vinegar
Remainder of tomato sauce

  Mix all ingredients and bring to a boil for 1 minute.
  Drain fat from the cooked meat loaf.
  Pour sweet and sour sauce over the meat loaf and bake another 10 minutes at 350°.

Sue's Sweet Potato Dinner

1 1/2 to 2 pounds sweet potatoes
4 green cooking apples
2 ham steaks (2 pounds)
1/2 cup apple juice or cider
4 teaspoons flour
2 tablespoons brown sugar

Peel and slice sweet potatoes.

Heat heavy skillet. In skillet, brown ham lightly on one side, turn, brown other side. Cut into bite-sized pieces.

Arrange potatoes around ham; cover tightly. Reduce heat and cook over low heat for 30 minutes, checking to see that potatoes don't stick.

While potatoes and ham are cooking, beat together apple juice and flour in a small bowl. Peel and slice apples.

Pour juice mixture around ham and cook, stirring carefully until thick.

Place the apple slices and brown sugar over potatoes and ham. Cover and cook another 10-15 minutes until apples are tender. This may serve 8 people.

*Y*our opportunity to
avoid dyspepsia
and other stomach
ailments will
be greatly enhanced if
you follow
these two simple rules:
    Eat slowly.
    Eat less.

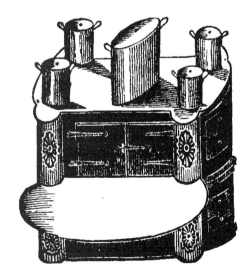

The dessert table gets a lot of attention from any church group. Despite dire warnings about sugar, chocolate, and fat, the goodies continue to disappear in record time.

I don't recall such warnings in my childhood; instead we were told, "Sweets to the sweet." This was good news unless, like Winnie, one wasn't allowed sweets of any kind. Winnie found the answer with this recipe.

Winnie's Banana Walnut Cake

2/3 cup mashed ripe bananas
1/2 cup butter or margarine
3 large eggs
3/4 cup water
2 cups flour
2 teaspoons baking powder
1 teaspoon soda
1 teaspoon cinnamon
1 cup chopped walnuts
1/2 cup raisins

Beat together mashed bananas and butter until creamy. Add eggs and water; beat well. Stir in flour, baking powder, soda, and cinnamon. Beat until smooth. Add walnuts and raisins.

Put in greased and floured 9" x 13" pan. Bake at 350° for 30-35 minutes or until knife comes out clean.

Poor Winnie occasionally went home without dessert because her cake was gone before she got to the table!

*H*eat nuts, fruits, and raisins in the oven before adding them to cake and pudding batter. They won't be as likely to settle to the bottom of the cake.

Sunday school picnic cooks have their loyal followers, and Grandma's daughter Claribel surely had hers. My "Aunt C.C.'s" chocolate cake was a winner.

"So light it floats off the fork!" "It doesn't get any better than this." "What do you mean it's all gone? I didn't get any!" These the comments heard regularly about her famous cake.

C.C. was ten years older than I, and everything she did was perfect in my eyes. She never fussed about having a little niece underfoot, and there were always tasty spoons and bowls to work on. I wasn't even banished from kitchen when her boyfriend came to supervise the cooking . . . so I was the witness one evening when they had a set-to over her chocolate cake.

C. C.'s Chocolate Cake

1 1/2 cups flour
1/2 cup cocoa
1/4 teaspoon salt
1 teaspoon soda
1 teaspoon baking powder
1 cup sugar
1/2 cup shortening
1 egg
1 teaspoon vanilla
1/2 cup sour milk
1/2 cup very hot water

Grease and flour a 9" x 13" pan or two round pans. Heat oven to 350°. Mix and sift first five dry ingredients.

Cream sugar and shortening until fluffy. Beat in egg, vanilla, and sour milk.

Add water to the dry mixture alternately with the creamed mixture. Beat well. Bake at 350° for 30-35 minutes.

Some women like to travel,
While others like a book.
But the woman who will get her man
Is the one who likes to cook!

When a cake is cooled and is stuck to the pan, place the pan on a damp towel for a few minutes. The cake will slide right out. Works for muffins, too.

Sid watched all this work with a cynical eye

"Why go to all that bother to put a cake together?" he wanted to know. "You take a lot longer than you need to."

"What do you know about it?" C. C. asked.

"I know I could turn out one as good as yours in half the time."

The challenge was accepted, the apron transferred, and Sid went to work. He dumped everything straight from the container to the bowl, stirred until he couldn't see the flour, and scraped it into the pans.

"It will be as flat as your hand and as heavy as a skillet," predicted C.C.

Judgment would come at the Sunday school picnic the next day. Would C.C.'s faithful fans be able to tell the difference between the two cakes? Sid thought not.

I licked both bowls and wisely refrained from taking sides.

You wonder how the contest ended? Try the recipe both ways and judge for yourself! (By the way, C.C. didn't marry Sid.)

She measured out
   the butter with a
   very solemn air,
The milk and sugar
   also;
She took the greatest
   care
To count the eggs
   correctly and to
   add a little bit
Of baking powder,
   which you know,
   beginners oft omit.
Then she stirred it all
   together
and she baked it full
   an hour,
But she never quite
   forgave herself
for leaving out the
   flour.

Mrs. Clark's Molasses Drop Cookies

Makes 64

1 cup shortening
1 cup sugar
1 cup molasses
2 eggs
2 teaspoons baking soda
1 cup sour milk
5 cups flour
3 teaspoons cinnamon
1 teaspoon ginger
1/2 teaspoon cloves
1 cup raisins
1 teaspoon salt

Cream shortening and sugar; add molasses. Beat eggs and add.
Dissolve soda in milk.
Sift together dry ingredients; add alternately with milk mixture to creamed mixture.
Drop by teaspoons on greased baking sheet.
Bake at 375° for 12 minutes.

*R*oll them, Drop
   them,
Press them in a pan.
Put them in the oven to
Bake to golden tan.

*W*arm cookies from
   the oven
There's nothing else to
   match
Alas! Tomorrow you'll
   have
To bake another batch.

Communion Bread

1/2 cup butter or margarine
1 cup flour
2 tablespoons sugar
milk to make soft dough

Cut the butter into the flour and sugar.
Add milk to make a soft dough and knead several times.
Chill the dough overnight.
Roll thin as a pie-crust. Score serving-size pieces. Bake at 375-400° for 10-12 minutes or until light brown on top. Watch carefully!

Potlucks and picnics weren't the only events for which the ladies of the church were held responsible. They also provided the communion bread for Sunday morning worship. All the ladies took a turn, using approximately the same simple recipe. The differences were evident only in the crispness, the degree of browning, and the shape of the pieces. Grandma scored her bread evenly, watched it carefully, and broke it precisely.

Jesus took the bread, gave thanks and broke it, and gave it to his disciples, saying, "Take and eat; this is my body."
Matthew 26:26

Tender, Loving Care

Every child experiences such things as measles, chicken pox, having tonsils out, or a bad cold that keep one housebound, if not right in bed. Probably most of us can remember a mother or grandma who provided love and extra goodies to "coax the appetite back."

Although these foods may have been served at other times, we remember best how good they tasted when we were first beginning to feel better.

In my childhood, eggs and milk were considered the principle ingredients for restoring health, and there were a lot of ways to put them together. None was a bigger success for me than Grandma's eggnog.

Food for thought is just like any other food. It should be properly prepared before serving.

Eggnog

Separate the egg carefully. Beat the white until it is almost stiff.

Beat the yolk until it is foamy, then add a little vanilla and a spoonful of sugar. Then beat cold milk into the yolk mixture until it is frothy.

Whirl in the egg white and add a little shake of nutmeg to the top.

This is not a sip-it-with-a-straw beverage; I drank it from a tall glass and licked off the mustache! It's a remedy that either cures you quickly—or prolongs the illness so you can have another!

Nothing takes the place of a cool hand on a hot forehead, but special taste treats for the sick one are cheering. And the further back you look to remember them, the more they seemed to have helped!

Long before pudding mixes could be purchased at the store, people enjoyed a variety of homemade custards. One that was smooth and silky to the taste and slid down a sore throat with great ease was junket. Plain junket didn't thrill me, but when Grandma added chocolate, I was happy to have some.

Chocolate Junket

1 cup milk, warmed slightly

1/4 Rennin (junket) tablet, dissolved in 1 tablespoon cold water

4 tablespoons cocoa powder

2 tablespoons sugar

1/4 teaspoon vanilla

Mix all ingredients and pour into two glass dishes; let stand in a warm place until it sets, then place in cooler to chill.

Orange Jelly

1 tablespoon granulated gelatin
1/4 cup cold water
1/2 cup boiling water
1/4 cup sugar
1 cup orange juice
1 tablespoon lemon juice

Soak the gelatin in 1/4 cup cold water until all the liquid is absorbed. Add the boiling water and sugar; stir until mixture is dissolved.

Stir in orange juice and lemon juice.

Let cool slightly, then add fruit if desired. Pour into dessert dishes and place in the cooler to become firm and cold.

Serve with whipped cream.

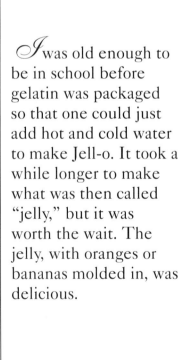

I was old enough to be in school before gelatin was packaged so that one could just add hot and cold water to make Jell-o. It took a while longer to make what was then called "jelly," but it was worth the wait. The jelly, with oranges or bananas molded in, was delicious.

Grandma always said that the worst part of being sick was getting better. I'm sure she was referring to that time when I didn't feel bad enough to want to stay in bed nor well enough to want to be up.

Life was easier for both of us when a basket on the bed held my dolls, coloring books and crayons, and the Sears Catalog. A small pair of scissors was all I needed to create a completely furnished doll house and a well-dressed family.

Meals were made easier by serving them in a muffin tin. There were enough compartments for food and even a small drinking glass. This cut down on the number of dishes that needed to be boiled, too.

Good Neighbor Recipe

1 tongue that does not slander
1 mind full of tolerance
2 ears closed to gossip
2 eyes overlooking others' faults
1 heart generous and kind
2 hands extended to help others
1 dash each of wit, sunny
disposition, and cheerfulness

Blend together all ingredients. Form into being; serve generous portions to everyone you meet daily.

A good neighbor doubles the value of a house.

The Sweet Things of Life

If Grandma had made only one kind of cookie while I was growing up, I would have chosen her sugar cookies over all the rest. They usually had scalloped edges and a sifting of sugar on top, but they could be cut into any shape for a holiday like Christmas or Valentine Day—and frosted and topped with candy sprinkles or chopped nuts. The important thing was the melt-in-your-mouth texture and the special taste.

There is still no cookie I would rather have.

This recipe is way over a hundred years old . . . from a time before lard and butter had become our enemies!

Grandma's Old-Fashioned Sugar Cookies

1/2 cup lard (solid shortening may be substituted)
1/2 cup butter or margarine
1 cup white sugar
1 cup brown sugar
4 eggs
3/4 cup canned milk
1/4 cup water
1 teaspoon vanilla
6 cups flour
3 teaspoons baking powder
1/4 teaspoon soda

Cream the lard, butter, and sugars together.
Beat the eggs and add milk, water, and vanilla.
Sift dry ingredients together.
Add to creamed mixture alternately with milk mixture.
Place the dough on a floured surface and roll out 3/8 inch thick.
Cut shapes with cookie cutter.
Bake at 350° for about 8 minutes. The bottom will be lightly browned, but the cookies will be white. Sprinkle with sugar or frost with powdered sugar icing.

The hardest dessert to turn down is something "I made especially for you."

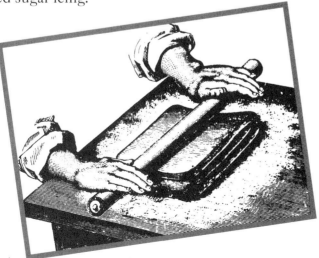

Aunt Violet, my grandma's sister, was another good cook in our family. One of her specialties was her sugar doughnuts. Fresh and warm and spicy, they were a symbol to me of happy hours together playing games, learning poems such as "Father William" and "The Old Gray Goose" or singing songs like "The Runaway Train" and "There Must Be Little Cupids in the Briny."

Aunt Violet and I also enjoyed popcorn evenings. She would pop a big bowl of corn, and we would settle down to enjoy it. As we munched, we lined up the "old maids," unpopped or partially popped kernels. Whoever had the most when the popcorn was gone was the winner!

Aunt Violet was a maverick in a family of fairly sedate individuals, and a mere whiff of a cinnamon sugar doughnut brings her back with all her outlandish fun that delighted her little grandniece!

Spiced Sugar Doughnuts

2 tablespoons shortening
1 cup sugar
2 eggs
4 1/2 cups flour
4 teaspoons baking powder
1 teaspoon salt
1 teaspoon nutmeg
1 cup milk
3/4 cup sugar
2 tablespoons cinnamon

Cream together shortening and 1 cup sugar.

Beat eggs and add to creamed mixture.

Sift flour, baking powder, salt, and nutmeg. Add dry ingredients and milk alternately to creamed mixture.

On floured surface, roll out 1/2 inch thick. Cut with a doughnut cutter. Fry in deep fat 3 minutes or until brown, turning once.

Drain on absorbent paper.

Mix remaining sugar and cinnamon. Shake warm doughnuts with cinnamon mixture in paper bag.

The first doughnut goes to the littlest person standing around.

Molasses Taffy

2 cups sugar

1/3 cup corn syrup

2/3 cup water

1 cup molasses

2 tablespoons butter

1 tablespoons vanilla

Cook the sugar, corn syrup, and water to 245°(soft ball when tested in cold water). Add the molasses and butter and cook to 260°(hard ball). Add vanilla.

Pour the mixture onto an oiled platter until cool enough to handle. Grease hands with butter and pull a ball of taffy between two people until it is very light colored and cold. Finally pull out into strips and cut in bite-size lengths.

Food coloring or flavoring other than vanilla may be swirled into the candy before it is turned out to cool. This will make variegated pieces that are attractive as well as yummy.

WARNING: Proceed with caution if you wear braces, retainers, or removable bridges!

We don't often hear about old-fashioned taffy pulls these days, but when Grandma was a young girl, they were an eagerly anticipated evening's entertainment. Not only was taffy fun to make, it had the added advantage of being good to eat before the party was over. A good fire in the range, a large kettle, and simple ingredients started things off.

Grandma didn't worry about sugar consumption the way we do. To adapt some of those sweet memories for our health-conscious ways, try these helpful tips.

- *Use less sugar in a recipe, but add a few grains of salt or extra vanilla.*

- *In cooking or baking, substitute 1/2 to 2/3 cup honey for each cup of sugar. Reduce the liquid called for by 1/4 cup. Lower the oven temperature by 25°, as honey has a browning effect on a baked product.*

- *A sprinkling of salt on a sour fruit like grapefruit makes it taste sweeter than spoonfuls of sugar!*

You Shall Live in the Land

Our grandfathers knew that the land held life. They knew that if the land was treated correctly, it would sustain the people who lived on it. In a society that was primarily agricultural, what the weather did, how one sowed, and how he reaped were of great importance. With practiced eye, farmers watched fields of wheat, rye, and oats, and knew when the time had come to harvest the fields. How well they understood the Scripture that says, "Remember this; whoever sows sparingly also reaps sparingly, and whoever sows generously will also reap generously" (II Corinthians 9:6).

Those who sow in
   tears
   will reap with songs
      of joy.
He who goes out
   weeping,
   carrying seed to sow,
will return with songs
   of joy,
   carrying sheaves
      with him.
Psalm 126:5, 6

I do not recall ever being on the farm during harvest season, but my friend Margaret vividly remembers those days in her childhood.

On the large farms in the Midwest, that time was exciting, especially if you were the daughter of the man who provided the thrashing crew for this important occasion.

Her father had a large threshing machine, powered by an equally large steam engine, with which he threshed thousands of acres of grain each year. His crew of eight included a cook, and his equipment was rounded out with a cook house! Drawn by a team of horses, the cook house followed the crew each day, and no king was ever fed more sumptuously than those men of the field. Margaret and her sister Ruth recall going out to the dusty fields early in the morning to help with this essential part of the harvest.

"We peeled potatoes, prepared vegetables, and carried ice water and lemonade to the men as they worked. The cook house was parked in the shade, and the sides of the wagon were let down to make tables for the meals. Papa provided for his crew from our own stores of meat, vegetables, and fruits."

In addition, good things were brought out from the farms being serviced, and every housewife had a "speciality" to offer the threshing crew. The men looked forward each year to these dishes.

Sow for yourselves righteousness, reap the fruit of unfailing love.

Hosea 10:12

Thelma's Harvest Pie

1 1/2 cups cooked winter squash

1/2 cup firmly packed brown sugar

1/2 teaspoon salt

1 teaspoon cinnamon

3 egg yolks

1 cup milk

2 tablespoons melted butter

1/2 cup chopped nut meats

9" unbaked pastry shell

3 egg whites

9 tablespoons sugar

Mash squash until free of lumps. Add brown sugar, salt, and cinnamon.

Beat egg yolks. Add milk, butter, and nut meats. Mix well.

Pour into pastry shell and bake at 400° for about 40 minutes or until filling is set and a silver knife inserted comes out clean.

Beat egg whites stiff, add sugar. Swirl meringue on top of the filling. Return to the oven to brown.

Sow a thought, and you reap an act;
Sow an act, and you reap a habit;
Sow a habit, and you reap a character;
Sow a character, and you reap a destiny.

Mildred's
Chicken and Egg Dumplings

Serves 16

4 large chickens, cut up
8 stalks celery, diced
4 medium onions, chopped
1 cup carrots, sliced
1 cup peas
1 1/2 cups milk
1 1/3 cups flour

Cover chicken with water. Season with salt and pepper.

Add celery and onion. Bring to boil, then simmer until tender (2 to 2 1/2 hours).

Remove bones and skin, skim off excess fat, and measure liquid. If necessary, add enough water to make 16 cups. Add vegetables.

Blend milk and flour, gradually add a little of hot liquid.

Stir into remaining hot liquid and cook, stirring until thickened.

Drop dumpling batter (page 50) by spoonfuls on top.

Cover tightly and simmer for 20 minutes without removing cover.

God gives every bird food, but He does not throw it into the nest.

J. W. Holland

Egg Dumplings

4 cups flour

6 teaspoons baking powder

2 teaspoons salt

8 egg yolks

1 1/3 cups milk

Sift together dry ingredients. Beat yolks with milk. Add to ingredients and mix lightly until blended.

Do not be deceived: God cannot be mocked. A man reaps what he sows . . . the one who sows to please the Spirit, from the Spirit will reap eternal life.

Galatians 6:7, 8

Cora's Cottage Pudding

Serves 12

1/2 cup butter

1 1/2 cups sugar

4 eggs

4 1/2 cups flour

1/2 teaspoon salt

6 teaspoons baking powder

1 1/2 cups milk

1 teaspoon lemon extract

Cream butter and sugar. Add eggs, one at a time, beating well after each.

Sift together flour, salt, and baking powder; add alternately with milk to creamed mixture.

Bake at 350° for 40 minutes. Serve hot with sauce.

Lemon Sauce
(Makes 3 cups)

2 tablespoons cornstarch
1 cup sugar
2 tablespoons grated lemon rind
salt—few grains
2 cups water
4 tablespoons lemon juice
4 tablespoons butter

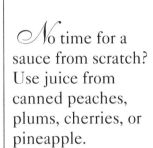

Mix cornstarch, sugar, lemon rind, and salt. Gradually add water. Cook over low heat, stirring constantly, until thickened. Cook in a double boiler 5 minutes. Add lemon juice and butter.

Serve over pudding, hot or cooled.

*N*o time for a sauce from scratch? Use juice from canned peaches, plums, cherries, or pineapple.

Thicken 1 cup of juice with 1 tablespoon of cornstarch (mixed with a little bit of water to prevent lumps).

Great over dry cake, apple dumplings, or waffles.

Tie a Ribbon 'Round the Memory

In Grandma's day, things were simpler. Not easier, perhaps, but less complicated.

Do you remember crusty snow sticking to wool mittens? The smell of wet socks steaming on the stove fender? Fingers too cold to unbuckle galoshes? Air so frigid it took your breath away?

Now, as I listen to the thermostat flip on the heat in the early morning, I recall the sound of ashes being shaken down in the kitchen range and the parlor stove as Uncle Roy lit the fires for Christmas Day. When I switch on the coffee maker and take rolls from the freezer, I can smell the ham sizzling in the black skillet and the cinnamon rolls browning in the wood-heated oven. I check the instructions on the frozen pie box and see the lineup of desserts on Grandma's kitchen dresser—pumpkin, mince, apple, and custard.

Try to pack these things into a ribbon-bedecked box! Fortunately we don't have to, because God's gift of memory has kept them securely with us. Smell, they say, is the best jogger of the memory. So sit awhile in the old farm kitchen, feeling the warmth, breathing in the delicious aroma, and remember. . . .

Those who are wrapped up in themselves make small packages.

Christmas cooking called for a lot of no-fuss, one-dish meals that could simmer on the back of the range or bubble in the oven while more important matters were cared for on the big table. One of my favorites, served with coleslaw, crusty bread, and a sample of whatever was baking that day, was Grandma's Five-Minute Special. I have discovered that in the West it is a variety of tamale pie—good by any name.

Grandma's Five-Minute Special

1 pound hamburger, browned
1 cup creamed corn
1 cup canned tomatoes
ripe olives

1 chopped green pepper
1/2 cup cornmeal
1 cup milk
grated cheese

Stir everything together except cheese; sprinkle that on top. Bake uncovered at 350° for one hour.

Those who have no Christmas in their hearts will never find Christmas under a tree.

On a day when there was left-over rice to warm in the top of the double boiler, C.C. often made drumsticks—a special favorite of mine. Stewed tomatoes, fruit, and cookies finished this quick-to-fix meal.

Drumsticks

2 pounds ground meat (beef, pork, veal)
1/2 cup chopped onion
1 cup fine dry bread crumbs
2 teaspoons prepared mustard

6 tablespoons fat
1 teaspoon salt
pepper to taste
2 eggs, beaten

Mix meat with onion, mustard, salt, and eggs.
Divide mixture into eight portions.
Shape each portion as a drumstick around a wooden skewer. Roll in bread crumbs.
Brown on all sides in hot fat. Reduce heat and continue to cook 15-20 minutes, turning occasionally.

Leah's Harvest Bars

1/2 cup sifted flour

1/2 teaspoon baking powder

1/4 teaspoon soda

1/2 teaspoon salt

1/2 teaspoon each cinnamon, nutmeg, ginger

1/2 cup shortening

1 cup brown sugar, firmly packed

2/3 cup cooked pumpkin, mashed

2 eggs

1/2 teaspoon vanilla

1/2 cup dates, chopped

1 tablespoon flour

1/2 cup walnuts, chopped

Sift together dry ingredients.

Melt shortening over a low fire and stir in brown sugar until well blended. Remove from heat and add pumpkin. Mix thoroughly, then add eggs one at a time, beating well. Add vanilla and blend in dry ingredients. Add floured dates and nuts.

Bake in a 9 x 9 x 2" pan for 30-35 minutes at 350°. Cut into bars and sprinkle with powdered sugar, or cut into squares and top with whipped cream for a great dessert, either warm or cold.

Could there be a proper Christmas celebration without cookies? Did you ever see, smell, or taste a store-bought cookie that could compete with one fresh from the oven? Christmas cookie recipes can be found in every women's magazine and cookbook. Fancy shapes and decorations can make ordinary cookies special for the season.

Good cooks have long known that a gift from the kitchen is among the most welcome. Grandma's friends and neighbors enjoyed this pretty holiday bread, accompanied by a copy of the recipe.

Festive Cranberry Bread

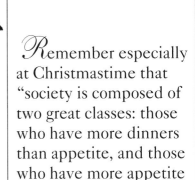

2 cups flour
1 cup sugar
1 1/2 teaspoon baking powder
1/2 teaspoon soda
1 teaspoon salt
1 egg, beaten
Juice and grated rind of 1 orange, plus 2 tablespoons shortening and enough boiling water to total 3/4 cup
1 cup each chopped walnuts and raw cranberries, halved

Sift the dry ingredients together. Blend in the egg and liquid; stir only until the flour mixture is dampened. Add nuts and cranberries.

Pour into a bread pan (8 1/2 x 4 1/2 x 3") or two miniature bread pans, pushing batter into corners of pan and leaving the center slightly hollow. Allow batter to stand in pan for 20 minutes before baking at 350° for 60-70 minutes.

Cool completely and frost.

Frosting for Cranberry Bread

1 1/2 cups powdered sugar
Add orange juice until frosting is good spreading consistency

When frosting is cool and dry, add "poinsettias" formed from mint gumdrop leaf candy and 1/2 candied cherry for each flower.

Sliced thinly for tea with butter or cream cheese, this bread is elegant! Toasted for breakfast, it's delicious! Have some ready to send home with visitors or carolers who show up at your door.

*R*emember especially at Christmastime that "society is composed of two great classes: those who have more dinners than appetite, and those who have more appetite than dinners" *(Chamfort)*.

As God's gift this year, may we not be a member of either class!

Peppermint was one of Grandma's favorite flavorings, and so of course it became mine, too. Tucked away in the corner of her handbag I could always find the little round white candies with XXXs on them to make sweet the moments of a long sermon. A soft cotton hanky with a drop of essence of peppermint comforted a stuffy nose. I can still hear myself saying, "Grandma, I need a peppermint hanky."

That wonderful fragrance and flavor even found its way into these best-of-all brownies.

Peppermint Brownies

1/2 cup shortening
1 cup sugar
2 eggs
1/2 teaspoon vanilla
2 1/2 squares of chocolate, melted and cooled
3/4 cup flour
1/2 teaspoon baking powder
1/2 teaspoon salt
1/2 cup chopped nuts
1/4 teaspoon peppermint flavoring

Cream shortening and sugar well. Add eggs, vanilla, and chocolate. Blend in dry ingredients and nuts. Mix well.

Pour into greased and floured 9 x 9 x 2" pan. Bake 25-35 minutes at 350°. Less baking time = chewier brownies!

*M*ice can't stand the smell of peppermint. Put fresh sprigs in corners or saturate a piece of cardboard with oil of peppermint, available at drug stores.

Peppermint Frosting

1 1/2 cups confectioner's sugar
light cream or evaporated milk
1-2 tablespoons soft butter
1/4 teaspoon peppermint flavoring
green food coloring

   Combine sugar and butter. Add milk by tablespoon; beat in to make good spreading consistency. Add peppermint flavoring and a drop of green food coloring, and beat until thick and creamy.
   Spread over cooled brownies. When firm, drizzle with 2 squares melted chocolate. Cut into squares and hide them in the cupboard—or stand back!

You say you need a diet more than
you need brownies?

Try the garlic sandwich diet.

You won't lose weight, but you'll seem smaller from a distance!

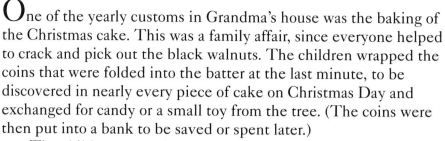

One of the yearly customs in Grandma's house was the baking of the Christmas cake. This was a family affair, since everyone helped to crack and pick out the black walnuts. The children wrapped the coins that were folded into the batter at the last minute, to be discovered in nearly every piece of cake on Christmas Day and exchanged for candy or a small toy from the tree. (The coins were then put into a bank to be saved or spent later.)

The children were also allowed to arrange the gumdrops on top of the cake in any way they chose, so the cake was decorated differently each year. I recall thumbprints that broke through the crispy top of the icing, but even with these—or perhaps because of them—the Christmas cake was the most beautiful creation of the year!

Grandma's Christmas Cake

1 cup butter
3 cups sugar
2 cups milk
5 cups cake flour
1 teaspoon vanilla
4 teaspoons baking powder
1/4 teaspoon salt
6 egg whites, beaten
2 cups cranberries, chopped
1 cup citron, chopped
1 cup black walnuts, chopped
coins wrapped in oiled paper

Beat the butter and sugar until very light and creamy. Add the milk alternately with four cups of the flour. Add vanilla and beat thoroughly.

Sift baking powder and salt into the last cup of flour; add to batter. Add the well-beaten egg whites.

Carefully fold in the cranberries, citron, black walnuts, and coins.

Bake about 40 minutes at 350° in three 9" layers. This will make a large cake. Frost with boiled icing.

Boiled Icing

1 1/2 cups sugar
1/2 teaspoon light corn syrup
2/3 cup boiling water
2 egg whites, stiffly beaten
1 teaspoon vanilla

Combine sugar, corn syrup, and water. Bring quickly to a boil, stirring only until sugar is dissolved. Boil rapidly, without stirring, until a small amount of syrup forms a soft ball in cold water.

Pour syrup in fine stream over egg whites, beating constantly. Add vanilla. Continue beating 10 to 15 minutes, or until icing is cool and of right consistency to spread.

Frost cooled cake and decorate with red and green gumdrops.

As Modern as Today

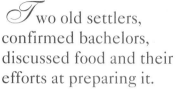

Modern equipment in the kitchen has changed the way mothers and grand-mothers cook today. For Grandma, a Calumet baking powder can with the bottom removed made an excellent biscuit or doughnut cutter. It was also used to chop potatoes for hash browns. Not many modern kitchens have a "spider" in them as Grandma's did—not the kind that made webs, of course, but a big cast-iron frying pan, so named because of its short feet that allowed it to stand among the coals on the open hearth.

Concerns for health and recent findings about certain foods have changed what people cook as well as how they cook it. Those of us who grew up eating anything that grew sometimes have difficulty with these changes.

We must accept the fact that changes come in all areas of our lives. But what a comfort to know that memories of good things do not change. The tastes, the aromas, and the good feelings of yester-day linger with us. The things that delighted us then delight us now.

Our lives are sustained, not only by good food, but by the knowl-edge that "God . . . richly provides us with everything for our enjoy-ment" (I Timothy 6:17 NIV). We are secure in the knowledge that, though all else in life becomes unsteady, "I the Lord do not change" (Malachi 3:6 NIV).

Now that should give us comfort!

Two old settlers, confirmed bachelors, discussed food and their efforts at preparing it.

Said one, "I got one o' them cookery books once, but I couldn't do nothin' with it."

"Too much fancy work in it, eh?"

"You said it. Every one o' them recipes began the same way: 'Take a clean dish . . .' and that settled me right there."

Here is a recipe for fun, if you feel like solving a puzzle while you bake.

Scripture Cake

1/2 cup NUMBERS 17:8
1 cup each I SAMUEL 30:12
2 cups GENESIS 18:6
3 ISAIAH 10:14, separated
1 1/2 cups JEREMIAH 6:20, KJV
1/2 cup PROVERBS 30:33
1/2 teaspoon I KINGS 10:10
1/2 teaspoon MATTHEW 5:13
2 teaspoons AMOS 4:5, KJV
1/2 cup GENESIS 24:11
1 tablespoon PROVERBS 24:13

Grease and flour the cake pan.

Chop figs, raisins, and almonds fine; flour them with part of 2 cups flour.

Beat egg whites until stiff and set aside.

Blend butter, sugar, spices and salt. Beat egg yolks and add. Sift in flour and fruits; beat well. Fold in egg whites.

Bake at 350° for 50-60 minutes.

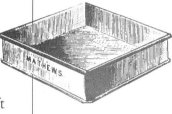

KEY TO
SCRIPTURE CAKE

Numbers 17:8 (almonds)
I Samuel 30:12 (raisins, figs)
Genesis 18:6 (flour)
Isaiah 10:14, separated (eggs)
Jeremiah 6:20, KJV (sugar)
Proverbs 30:33 (butter)
I Kings 10:10 (cinnamon, mace, cloves)
Matthew 5:13 (salt)
Amos 4:5 KJV (baking powder)
Genesis 24:11 (water)
Proverbs 24:13 (honey)

*M*any fine things can be done in a day, if you don't make that day tomorrow.

*W*orry, like a rocking chair, will give you something to do, but it won't get you anywhere.

Twelve Hints
to Help a Kitchen Master

1. For lumpless gravy, add a pinch of salt to the flour before mixing it with water.

2. Scald tomatoes, peaches, or pears in boiling water before peeling. Skins will slip right off.

3. Meat loaf will not stick to a metal pan if you place a slice of bacon in the bottom of the pan.

4. Muffins will slide right out of tin pans if the pan is first placed on a wet towel.

5. No sticking to the pan when you're scalding milk if you first rinse the pan in cold water.

6. A lump of butter or margarine added to water will prevent rice, noodles, or spaghetti from boiling over.

7. A few drops of lemon juice added to simmering rice will keep the grains separate.

8. Is this egg hard boiled? Spin it. If it wobbles and won't spin, it's raw. If it spins, it is hard.

9. A dampened paper towel or terry cloth brushed downward on a cob of corn will remove every strand of corn silk.

10. Eggshells are easily removed from hard-boiled eggs if eggs are quickly rinsed in cold water first.

11. Scorched the inside of your favorite pan? Don't panic. Fill it halfway with water, add 1/4 cup soda, and boil until burned portions loosen and float to the top.

12. A jar lid or a couple of marbles in the bottom of a double boiler will rattle when the water gets low and warn you to add more.

For more warm memories of days gone by,
you'll enjoy Arleta Richardson's
Grandma's Attic Series:

❧

In Grandma's Attic

More Stories from Grandma's Attic

Still More Stories from Grandma's Attic

Treasures from Grandma

Sixteen and Away from Home

Eighteen and on Her Own

Nineteen and Wedding Bells Ahead

At Home in North Branch

New Faces, New Friends

Stories from the Growing Years

The Grandma's Attic Storybook